# AMERICAN INVENTIONS

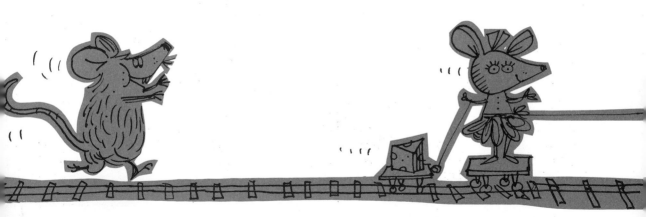

# AMERICAN

Holt, Rinehart and Winston

New York / Chicago / San Francisco

A BOOK TO BEGIN ON

# INVENTIONS

By Leslie Waller

Illustrated by Ed Emberley

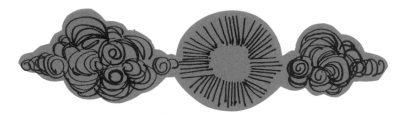

Published simultaneously in Canada by Holt, Rinehart
and Winston of Canada, Ltd.

Library of Congress Catalog Card Number: 63–15139

SBN: 03–041265–x

Printed in the United States of America

When America was first discovered, people called it the "New World." They came here from many lands and found many new things to learn and do.

Life in the New World was hard at first. So people began to invent ways to make life easier.

In this way, a wonderful story began: the story of American inventions.

In the early days of America people couldn't just go to the store for a loaf of bread.

First, they had to plant wheat grain. After the wheat grew, farmers cut it down. From wheat they made flour for bread.

The first American invention we know about had to do with wheat. In the colony of Massachusetts, in 1646, a man named Joseph Jenks invented a new machine to make scythes for cutting wheat.

A scythe is a long curved knife. The farmer swings it with both hands to cut down stalks of wheat.

Today we know about Joseph Jenks's invention because he got a "patent" on it.

A patent is something an inventor gets from the government of his country.

He tells the government about his new invention. He draws pictures of it. He shows how it works.

If there is nothing exactly like it, the government gives him a patent.

Joseph Jenks got a patent on his new way to make scythes. The patent was a piece of paper that told everyone:

"Joseph Jenks owns this invention. If you want to use it, you must ask him to let you. If he doesn't let you, then you can't use it. It is against the law to use his invention unless he lets you."

When America was young there were many other inventions, because so many were needed.

Men had to carry guns to protect their families and hunt for food. Because guns were so needed, people wanted to make them better. An important early American invention was an extra-long rifle. With it, a man could hit a target that was very far away.

Gunmakers who had come to America from Germany and Switzerland invented this rifle. It was used a lot in Kentucky by people like Daniel Boone. Today we call it the "Kentucky Long Rifle."

Most people remember Benjamin Franklin as one of the early leaders of our country.

But he was also one of our best-known inventors.

He enjoyed sitting in one of his own inventions: the rocking chair.

He invented many other things, too.

Most fireplaces in America used to be made of stone or brick. They burned up the wood very fast. Often, they filled the houses with smoke.

In 1742, Ben Franklin invented a kind of iron fireplace rather like a small stove. It burned wood slowly and gave a great deal of heat. It also did a good job of keeping smoke out of a room. Today, we still call this invention the "Franklin stove."

Franklin was very interested in lightning. He knew how dangerous it could be. If it hit a house, he knew it could start a fire.

So Franklin invented the "lightning rod." This is a pointed metal rod put on the highest part of a house. A thick wire runs from the rod to the ground.

When lightning strikes, it usually hits the highest part of a house. If lightning hits the rod, it can flow down the wire and into the ground. That way it can't hurt the house or anyone inside it.

There were many more early American inventors. One was a schoolteacher from New England, Eli Whitney. After the colonies had won their freedom from England, Whitney went South to teach in the state of Georgia.

Cotton was an important crop in Georgia. There are two kinds of cotton. One has long fibers. Its seeds are easy for the farmers to pick out and throw away.

But cotton with short fibers has seeds that are hard to pick out. As the pioneer farmers moved west, they found the land would grow only short-fiber cotton.

Was there an easier way of picking the seeds out of this cotton?

In 1793, Whitney invented a "cotton gin."

Inside the gin were little hooks that tore seeds out of the short-fiber cotton.

People put raw cotton in the machine and turned a crank. Out came cotton without seeds.

This worked much faster than the old way of picking the seeds out by hand.

Because the cotton gin saved time and money, people grew short-fiber cotton all over the South. It is still an important and useful product.

Our country began to grow faster. As people moved farther west, inventions were needed to help them travel greater distances in less time.

John Fitch of Connecticut built a boat that worked by means of a steam engine.

His boat had twelve oars. Instead of men having to row with the oars, an engine did the work. The boat looked like a huge waterbug scooting along the river.

But it didn't move very fast, and it kept breaking down.

Then, in 1807, Robert Fulton launched his invention: the first "steamboat" that worked really well.

It used a paddlewheel instead of oars or a sail. It moved fast, and it didn't break down very often.

Fulton's first steamboat was called the *Clermont*. It took people on trips up and down the Hudson River in New York.

Steam was used for other inventions, too. Until 1831, people cut wheat by hand with scythes. This took a long time to do. Many inventors tried to make a machine to harvest wheat.

Then, in 1831, Cyrus McCormick and a Negro slave, Jo Anderson, finally built a "mechanical reaper." A steam engine could be attached to such a reaper, or it could be pulled by horses. Big blades that looked like paddlewheels chopped down the wheat.

The "McCormick reaper" worked as fast as six men could work with scythes.

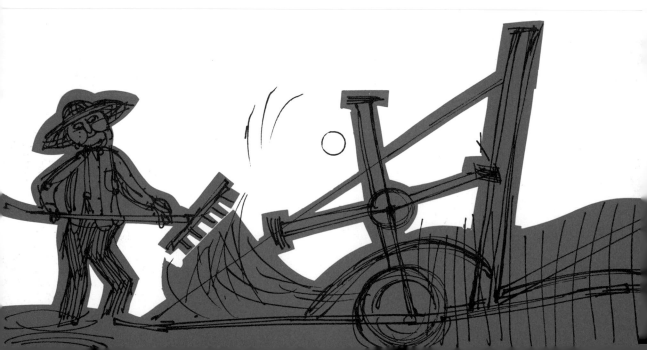

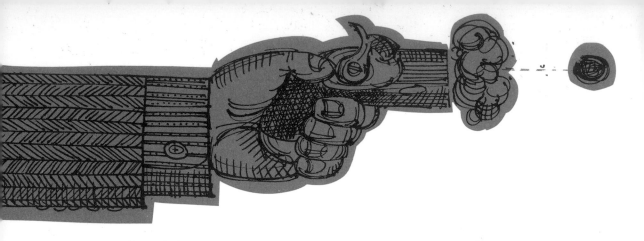

In the new lands to the west the country was filled with wild animals, bandits, and Indians. Men had to carry guns to protect themselves.

Henry Deringer invented a gun so small it could be hidden in a man's clothes. Until then, many guns were very big and heavy, like the Kentucky Long Rifle.

This small gun took the name of its inventor. Today, we call it a "derringer." It has one more "r" than Henry's last name had.

Another man gave his name to the gun he invented. This was Samuel Colt. In 1835, he invented a gun that shot six times without reloading. The "Colt six-shooter" became the gun most often used out West.

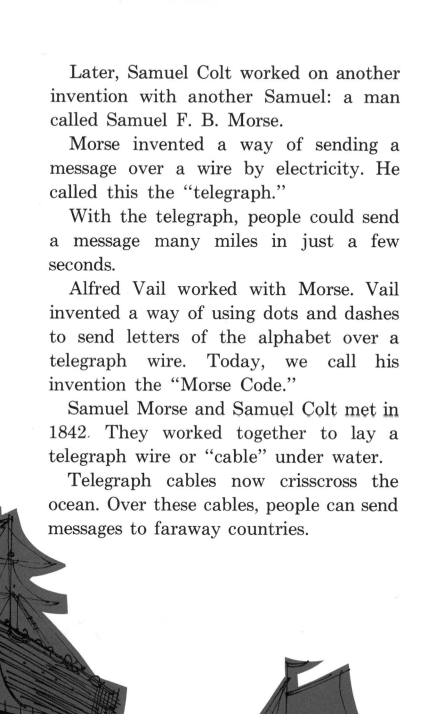

Later, Samuel Colt worked on another invention with another Samuel: a man called Samuel F. B. Morse.

Morse invented a way of sending a message over a wire by electricity. He called this the "telegraph."

With the telegraph, people could send a message many miles in just a few seconds.

Alfred Vail worked with Morse. Vail invented a way of using dots and dashes to send letters of the alphabet over a telegraph wire. Today, we call his invention the "Morse Code."

Samuel Morse and Samuel Colt met in 1842. They worked together to lay a telegraph wire or "cable" under water.

Telegraph cables now crisscross the ocean. Over these cables, people can send messages to faraway countries.

Not all United States inventions were used to link places that were far apart. In 1849, Walter Hunt just linked two pieces of cloth.

He did this with a piece of wire he had twisted into a new shape. In this way he invented a pin that stayed pinned.

He called it the "safety pin."

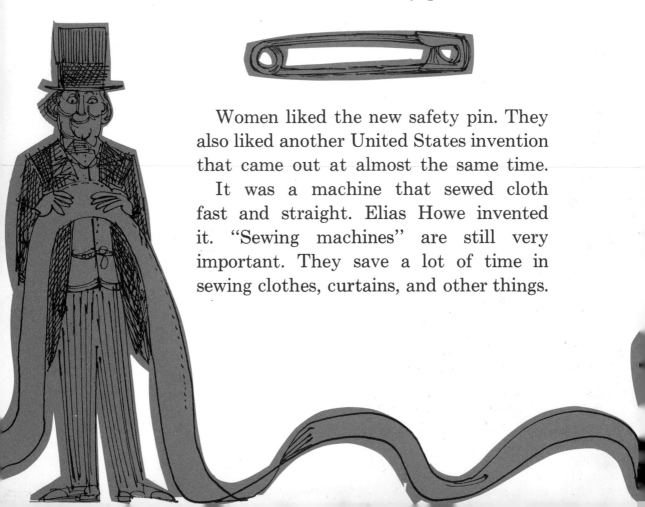

Women liked the new safety pin. They also liked another United States invention that came out at almost the same time.

It was a machine that sewed cloth fast and straight. Elias Howe invented it. "Sewing machines" are still very important. They save a lot of time in sewing clothes, curtains, and other things.

For many years the clothing that people wore was fastened with buttons, hooks, and pins.

A United States inventor named Whitcomb Judson changed that. He made two metal chains that slid together and hooked.

He first showed his invention in 1893. Today, we call it the "zipper."

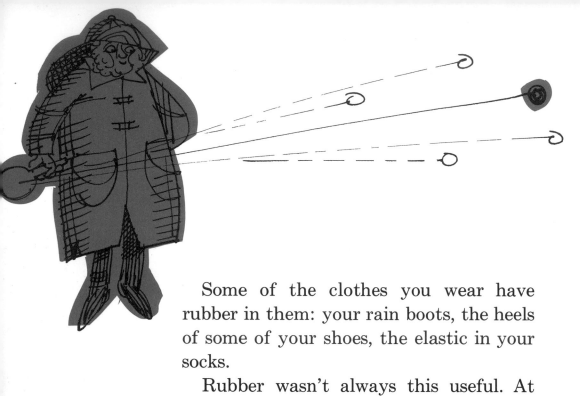

Some of the clothes you wear have rubber in them: your rain boots, the heels of some of your shoes, the elastic in your socks.

Rubber wasn't always this useful. At one time it was sticky and hard to work with, sort of like chewing gum.

Then a United States inventor, Charles Goodyear, found a way to make rubber easier to use. Today, we use Goodyear's kind of rubber for many things, including pencil erasers and auto tires. His way of making rubber useful was called "vulcanization."

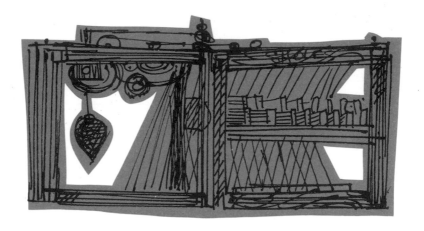

After the Civil War, United States inventors began to make many new things that were useful in offices.

Christopher Sholes invented the "typewriter" in 1868. Another way to write—the "fountain pen"—was invented in 1884 by Lewis Waterman. Before the fountain pen was made, pens had to be dipped in ink after every few written words.

The "cash register" you see in stores
was invented by James Ritty in 1879.
William Burroughs invented a machine
that could add. Today you see a kind of
"adding machine" on the check-out
counter at the market.

Elisha Otis invented a little car that
took people up and down in office
buildings. It was called an "elevator."

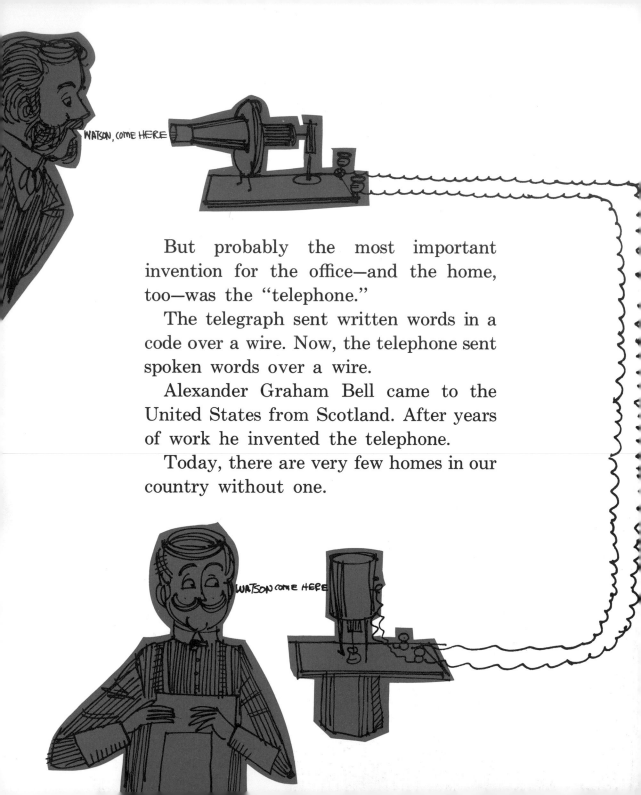

But probably the most important invention for the office—and the home, too—was the "telephone."

The telegraph sent written words in a code over a wire. Now, the telephone sent spoken words over a wire.

Alexander Graham Bell came to the United States from Scotland. After years of work he invented the telephone.

Today, there are very few homes in our country without one.

Another very important United States invention was made by another man who came here from a foreign country.

Ottmar Mergenthaler was a German watchmaker. After he came to the United States, he changed the way books, magazines, and newspapers were printed.

Until Mergenthaler's invention, each letter was printed from a single piece of type. Printers put the type together by hand. It took a long time.

Mergenthaler invented the "Linotype." It set a whole line of words at one time.

In the last century people had no electric or gas refrigerators. Milk and other food could not be kept fresh for very long.

So, in 1853, Gail Borden invented the process for "condensing" milk. Some years later, John Meyenberg invented a way to make "evaporated" milk.

Both kinds of milk could be sealed in cans. The milk stayed fresh for a long time that way.

Later, electric and gas refrigerators made another United States invention possible.

Your mother sometimes gives you "quick-frozen" foods. These were frozen when fresh. They stay fresh until they are defrosted and ready to eat.

Clarence Birdseye invented quick-frozen food in 1925. Now, it is eaten all over the world.

In the last century people rode thousands of miles by railroad. Trips took many days. People slept in their clothes, sitting in uncomfortable seats.

An American inventor named George Pullman, decided to make something that would let people go to sleep in a bed while riding on the train.

He invented a kind of folding bed. Now, people could change into their nightclothes and have a good night's sleep as they traveled in what are still called "Pullman cars."

Until 1888, cameras were big, heavy things. People took pictures on special sheets of glass. The glass sometimes broke.

Then, George Eastman invented a small camera that was easy to use. It didn't need glass plates. It used a "roll" of film.

Today, almost all cameras use roll film. Some cameras are so small you can hide one in your hand.

Some United States inventors made more than one invention. The man who made more than any other was Thomas Alva Edison.

Of all his many inventions you probably know two best. They may be near you now as you read this book.

One is the "electric light."

The other is the "phonograph."

Edison invented them both, but he didn't stop at that. There are more than thirteen hundred patents on the inventions he made!

What else would United States inventors think of?

For centuries men had tried to fly. They failed. But two American brothers, Wilbur and Orville Wright, changed that.

On December 17, 1903, on a hill in Kitty Hawk, North Carolina, they tried out a new invention. Orville rode in the machine. It rose into the air and flew 120 feet!

The Wright brothers called their invention the "airplane." With it, man could finally fly.

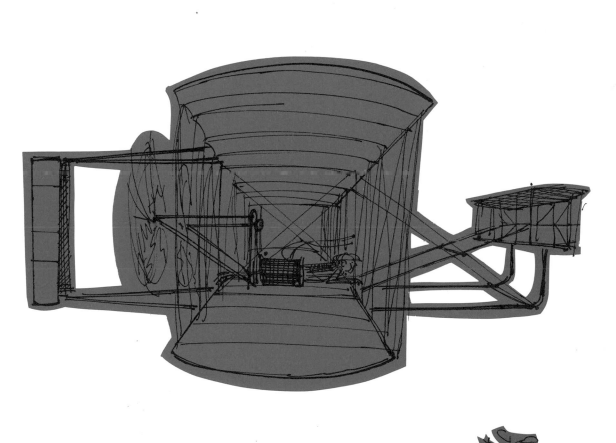

"Radio" was invented by an Italian, Guglielmo Marconi. It was a way of sending Morse code dots and dashes through the air without wires.

Voices and music could not yet be sent through the air this way. A number of United States inventors worked on the idea of doing that.

Lee De Forest, Edwin Armstrong, and Philo Farnsworth were among them. Their ideas finally developed the kind of radio we listen to today.

Some of these inventors helped to create television, too.

The picture tube you look at in your television set is called a "kinescope."

It was invented by an American who came here from Russia, Vladimir Zworykin.

Many inventors helped to make today's space "rockets." Among the first was an American named Robert H. Goddard.

Back in 1926, he had already invented rockets that used liquid fuels, the way many of today's rockets do.

Goddard also invented a rocket that would blast off with another rocket riding on top: the "two-stage rocket."

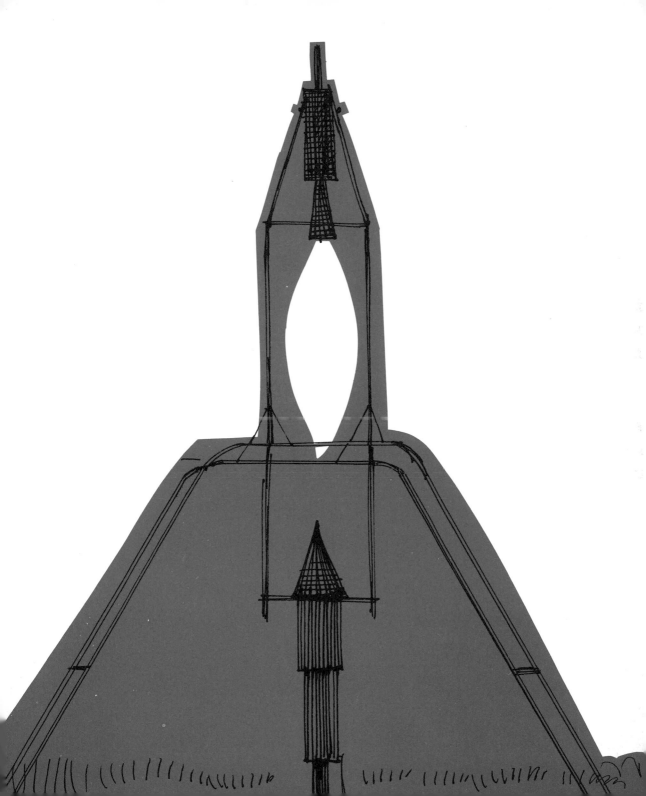

"Computers" are electrical machines that solve problems. Some people call them "thinking machines."

Computers of all kinds are hard at work today helping scientists solve many problems.

One of the first electronic computers was invented in 1945 by two Americans, John Mauchly and John Eckert, Jr.

People say, "Necessity is the mother of invention."

A necessity is something we need to live in the world. When an inventor recognizes a need, it makes him think of an invention to meet it.

Right now, the world needs many things: more food for billions of people, new ways to reach outer space, water for our deserts, new ways to make power when we use up our coal and oil supply.

Inventors all over the world are working to meet those needs. Maybe you will do so with your invention some day.

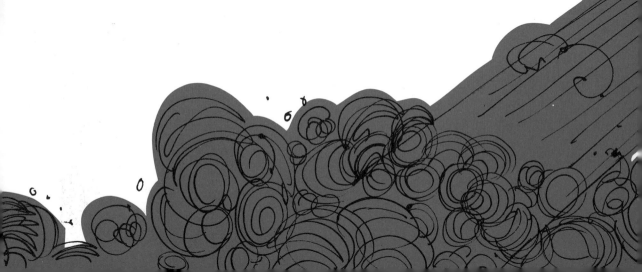

The author of six successful novels for adults, Leslie Waller recognizes the need for accurate, intelligent, expository books on historical and scientific subjects for beginning readers. He is the well-known author of several titles in the *Books to Begin On* series. A graduate of the University of Chicago, with an M.A. from Columbia University, Mr. Waller is an executive with a public-relations firm in New York City, where he lives with his wife and two young daughters.

Ed Emberley is a free-lance artist whose first book for children, *The Wing on a Flea,* was chosen by the New York *Times* as one of the best illustrated children's books of 1961. A graduate of the Massachusetts School of Art, he lives in a magnificent early American house on a tidal river off Boston's North Shore. In the small barn attached to the house Mr. Emberley prints limited editions of children's books on his own press, and is looking for a big old hand press to expand his operations.

608.7
W

Waller, Leslie

A book to begin
on American
inventions

| DATE | | | |
|---|---|---|---|
| JAN 29 | 2 9 | 2 15 | |
| | 211 | 217 | |
| MAY 25 | 222 | | |
| 5-W J | DEC 19 | 215 | |
| 5-W | 18 | | |
| 30 | 2 | | |
| APR 4 | | | |
| 113 | 14 | | |
| 109 | 216 | | |
| 112 | 215 | | |
| 35 | 217 | | |
| 32 | 214 | | |

© THE BAKER & TAYLOR CO.